The
COMFORTS
of HOME

ALSO BY MERRITT IERLEY

Open House:
A Guided Tour of the American Home, 1637 to the Present

Traveling the National Road:
Across the Centuries on America's First Highway

With Charity for All:
Welfare and Society, Ancient Times to the Present

The Year That Tried Men's Souls:
A Journalistic Reconstruction of the World of 1776

A Place in History:
A Centennial Chronicle of North Arlington, New Jersey,
Birthplace of Steam Power in America